What We Can Do

MARK LANDAU

DEDICATION

To us all

CONTENTS

ACKNOWLEDGMENTS

To my dear friends Marshall Hirsch, Umi,
Aaron Bohrer, Shannon White and Susan Herring
for their love, inspiration, input and support.

FORWARD

The sun will stand as your best man
And whistle
When you have found the courage
To marry Forgiveness
When you have found the courage
To marry Love
~~Hafiz (as translated by Daniel Ladinsky in The Gift)

On November 26, 2008, my husband and only daughter were killed by terrorists in the Oberoi Hotel in Mumbai, India. Naomi was thirteen. After a painful period of shock and mourning, I realized that, for me, the only thing to do was to love and forgive the people who did this. When I saw the face of the lone surviving terrorist, a very confused young man, I saw there was already too much fear and hate. We must send love and compassion. The most compassionate and loving thing to do is to forgive. Forgiveness is an act of love that generates more love. It is the bridge to peace.

I then began a long journey of research and analysis to try to understand why areas of humanity are continually using violence for ends that a peaceful society shuns. Since then, love and forgiveness have become my keystones because they bring me the most strength and nourishment. The more I have put this into practice, the more I have healed myself from this horrific loss. Healing restores balance and wholeness. I came to life all over again in a way I never imagined. As Mark says,

"Love and forgiveness are the foundation stones for acceptance, tolerance, compassion and benevolence and even understanding, faith and surrender—all the positive agents of progress and healing."

This book is a powerful gift that provides a simple and effective tool for transforming any kind of darkness into light. It is a key to open our hearts so that we may experience the love that we are, that is our very nature and that is aching to flow out of us into a world that has forgotten what is most important for our evolution as a human race.

I believe this book and the Love and Forgiveness Meditation it contains are ideal adjuncts to all the work I have been doing to counter-balance terrorism since the death of my husband and daughter. It will help many people develop the most beneficial qualities in their lives. I plan to offer *What We Can Do* as a companion to my *Pocketbook of Peace*.

To respect the dignity of life in all, we must love and forgive on a daily basis. This will keep our connection to each other alive. When we feel that connection, we cannot harm one another. We will find ways to resolve our differences. A profound contribution to world peace is to practice the Love and Forgiveness Meditation. By transforming ourselves, we transform the world. It's what we can do, as Mark so eloquently outlines for us in this remarkable little book.

Kia Scherr

President and Co-founder of One Life Alliance, a global peace initiative

www.onelifealliance.org

PREFACE

I offer this new healing meditation to you and all who may be inspired to look into and try it.

It did for me what forty-nine years of utilizing, teaching and facilitating other meditations and healing modalities didn't.

My hope is that the ideas and the practical tool herein will help you and others heal, reclaim your wholeness and more fully actualize all you are.

We need a new, better way of being.

Our world cries out for it.

This could help bring it about.

God bless and all good wishes,

Mark Landau
Santa Fe, NM
May 18, 2015

1. THE BASIS OF LIFE

Underlying all we are is something so subtle, quiet and close that we rarely perceive it.

The sages have tried to point to it knowing that no words would do.

It is silence, peace, contentment; innate, divine intelligence; eternal, vast awareness; the empty, effulgent void; the vacuum state of Quantum Mechanics; incorruptible invincibility; the core of what we are; the source of all that is.

It carries the qualities of love, support and harmony; acceptance, benevolence and oneness; wholeness, truth and freedom.

It is real.

It's a quality, a feeling, a vibration and beyond all these.

It's the basis of life.

It feeds and sustains everything.

It is beyond manipulation.

It is sanctity/consciousness/bliss, the love-glue that holds the atom and galaxy together.

It is worth cultivating, though few know how or care to.

It is more important than anything else because it enriches everything.

The more we bring it forth, the more we help every aspect of life.

It's already here, but we can more fully live it.

Nothing helps more to bring this about than a daily practice of meditation.

Nothing is more important.

The more we cultivate the basis of life, the more it leads us into living our highest good.

The more we live our highest good, the more we contribute to the highest good of our loved ones and the world.

We can and must transform our lives.

Our survival could depend on it.

2. THE VALUE OF MEDITATION

Over the eons millions of us have come to hold meditation as our dearest practice.

The Dalai Lama said, "If every eight-year-old in the world is taught meditation, we will eliminate violence from the world within one generation."

But it goes beyond this.

Meditation *can* heal the vicious cycle of assault and retaliation.

It can neutralize the rage, fear, control, angst, shame, guilt, depression, addiction, murder, suicide and war that characterize so much of our world.

But it can also increase our direct experience of love, peace, creativity, joy and freedom. It can harmonize our lives and allow us to interact more smoothly with others and the world. It can replace hurting and being hurt with loving and being loved, with thriving and helping others to thrive.

We eat three times a day. We wash our hands, mouths and bodies.

Let's wash our minds, hearts and souls of the damage life is heir to.

If we're lucky, people will someday marvel at the time when so few practiced the inner hygiene of daily meditation as we now may marvel at the time when raw sewage flowed along our city streets.

We live in barbaric times.

Each person who starts meditating begins to carry their weight like never before. They uplift the human race. They add more peace and actualization to our world and diminish turmoil and dysfunction.

Together we augment this influence.

Meditation also develops our perceptual abilities, our discernment, our comprehension and our being.

It is a vehicle of awareness, the basis of our experience. It develops and deepens awareness and experience. It can also awaken the endless richness of our spiritual dimensions. It fans the divine spark within and helps us see and live our oneness.

This allows us to accept our differences as a natural part of the kaleidoscopic variety of life in a world that can support us all. It heals our hate, intolerance and bigotry, for all hate stems from suppressed self-hatred.

It dissolves our separation and reconnects us with all that is.

It usually does these things slowly over time. But it can precipitate huge breakthroughs.

We are all transmitters and receivers. We broadcast what we live. And innumerable influences flow through us all the time.

If we're agitated or unhappy, that's what we give and receive. If we're loving, calm and peaceful, we spread that everywhere we go.

When we meditate, our vibratory patterns change. Whether we realize it or not, we settle into deeper states of being. Our metabolism slows down. Our system comes to rest.

This allows us to attain deeper harmony, access greater levels of power and heal some of our malaise.

Doing this three times a day brings grace to our own lives and all we touch.

Meditation doesn't do everything, but it's our best tool.

It's the lifeline for a species spinning out of control and plunging deeper into corruption, suppression and the degradation of all we hold dear.

The more of us doing this one simple thing, the more chance we have of pulling ourselves out of the quagmire.

It won't take vast numbers of us to make an impact.

Each one who starts to diminish the dark pushes the envelope into the light.

Join us in this sacred endeavor.

3. SIMPLICITY AND POWER

At the root of creation are simplicity and power.

Over a century ago Einstein divined his formula relating matter, energy and the speed of light.

It both defined and reflected the hidden order within all we see around us.

Everyone knows it as $E=MC^2$.

What it means is that energy and mass, or matter, are equal. Matter is made of energy. And every particle of matter contains a vast amount of energy, specifically, the amount of mass times C squared, C standing for Celeritas, Latin for speed, here meaning the speed of light.

This number is huge. It's around 300 million meters per second or a billion feet per second. When squared it's exponentially larger.

All the energy released from an atom would kill a flea. All the energy released from a gram of matter, about the mass of a paper clip, would flatten a city.

This is the simplicity and power of every particle of creation.

By simplicity, I don't mean easy to understand or accept. It's not. It's mind boggling and unfathomable. It flies in the face of all our perceptions. How could a table be nothing but energy and contain enough to decimate a continent? It's crazy, yet true. And since it is, the whole world is not as we perceive.

At the core of existence are a few key elements—energy, matter and the speed of light—that are in a relationship so simple it can be defined by $E=MC^2$. It goes beyond comprehension.

When it comes to Einstein's General Theory of Relativity, relating gravity and the energy and momentum of matter and radiation in the curvature of space-time, it's a bit more complicated.

$$G_{\mu\nu} + \Lambda g_{\mu\nu} = \frac{8\pi G}{c^4} T_{\mu\nu}$$

But when you think of what it encapsulates and the cartoons of physicists covering chalkboards with formulas, it again is astonishingly simple.

What this shows is that we can unearth the underlying principles and unleash the power inherent in the fundamental nature of our universe. At the basis of our physical world are elegance, simplicity and power.

I'm no Einstein, but I do feel that through grace and a lifelong desire to heal myself and others, I was gifted a simple formula for healing.

So I'm not being totally facetious when I type $H=M(L+F)^n$.

Healing equals Meditation multiplied by the power of Love and Forgiveness to the nth degree.

At the root of our inner world are a few key elements—awareness, love and forgiveness—that form a relationship which can, through meditation, unleash great healing power.

Awareness is the basis of all our experience. And meditation is the most effective tool for focusing and channeling it.

Love and forgiveness are the foundation stones for acceptance, tolerance, compassion and benevolence and even understanding, faith and surrender—all the positive agents of progress and healing.

In a way, awareness is like energy, love is like matter and forgiveness is like the speed of light—elusive, counter-intuitive and difficult to understand, utilize and accept.

Most people shy away from it.

"Why is it necessary?"

"What is there to forgive, forgive who? I've done nothing to need forgiveness."

But think about it. Can we forgive ourselves for all our weaknesses and foibles, all the damage we have given and received? Can we forgive God, the universe, our parents, siblings, partners and children, our school systems, politicians, governments and corporations, the lords of money and the unutterable, criminal stupidity of our own human arrogance for all the slings and arrows of outrageous fortune—all the circumstances of our lives and the world we would have otherwise?

Can we forgive the tribes, sects and ethnic groups we perceive as our enemies?

In the end, we must forgive everything—all the illusions, delusions and demands of reality—if we are to have peace.

Forgiveness doesn't mean we stop trying to improve things. It liberates us from the bondage of antagonism, of seeing ourselves as separate.

We have great resistances to the beauty of unity and freedom. It is at the deeper levels of meditation where our inherent wisdom can work wonders.

When I ask people to meditate with the mantra "I love you and forgive you," their knee jerk response is often, "That's too simple. What could that do?"

In its simplicity and utilization of the most fundamental healing elements lies its power.

I also hear, "I'm pretty well-adjusted. I'm not sick. I don't need healing."

While I *am* speaking of the healing unhealthy people might need, I refer to far more than this.

We all live innumerable limitations. They are mostly subconscious and come to us through our cultures, our families, our ancestries, our past lives and the world.

We are hardwired this way. That's what the ego is for, to keep us small and spinning. We carry so many traumas we are not aware of. The sins of our forbears come down all the generations. Our limitations rule us more than we know.

Ultimately, in one life or another, they must be healed and released.

While our shadow material is vast, most of it can go without our even knowing.

But sometimes chunks arise to be consciously looked at, acknowledged, owned, processed, healed and released.

Fifty years ago we spoke of using a small percent of our mental potential. But it's more than this.

We are eternal, multi-dimensional beings living a limited, human existence.

Healing allows us to live more of the fullness we truly are.

I'm not saying my formula is the only way. Nor am I saying that everyone will take to it. But when I combined the mechanics of deep meditation with love and forgiveness, profound things happened that didn't in my forty-nine other years of pursuing wholeness.

I can't help but believe this could benefit others.

Yet mostly what I see when I offer this is immediate, silent dismissal.

("Oh yeah, meditation. Maybe for you, not for me." Or, "Been there, done that." Or, "Right, next item, please.")

Perhaps this is our ego trying to circumvent our growing beyond our smallness.

Let's open the doors of possibility.

God knows we need something.

4. LOVE AND FORGIVENESS

It's like water.

Nothing beats it for cleansing and hydrating. Contrary to appearance, we are mostly made of water.

Just like that, love and forgiveness are the two best healing agents. Contrary to experience, we are mostly made of love. And forgiveness is essential. The two combined can do more for us than we know. And I'm not talking about some saccharine mood. I'm referring to their essential nature, vibration, elemental qualities, their power when we activate them at the deepest levels of our being.

They can clear the negative influences that drive our behavior.

But we can't just create love and forgiveness at will.

Our bodies contain about a hundred trillion cells. Each cell has a similar number of atoms. One big toenail contains the energy of an atom bomb. But we can't consciously access that power.

Similarly, everywhere we go we carry love and forgiveness. They are a basic part of the energy we are made of. But we can't consciously access their power.

Meditation allows our awareness to dive into the deeper levels of creation where reside the simplicity and power that underlie all things. This occurs automatically, usually without our realizing. Our inner wisdom can then take over and deliver the healing power of love and forgiveness to the places within us that need it most.

When we cut ourselves, we don't consciously heal the cut. It just happens. We take the precautions of cleaning and protecting it. Our healing capability then does the rest.

When we meditate with love and forgiveness, we set up the preconditions for our deeper healing to take place. Our higher power knows how to bring this about. But we need these quiet, deeper times to give it the chance. This can't really happen when we're running errands, self-medicating or being entertained.

These quiet times end up serving us far more than anything else our conscious minds can come up with. And the healing happens beyond our doing.

I believe we are basically decent. But our lives and impulses can be distorted and impelled into corrupt behavior through our damage and conditioning.

We live a fallen state. When this is healed, we find our true nature—forgiveness, acceptance, freedom, happiness, creativity and the innate ability to love and support all we are and all that is.

5. DOING IT

So how do we get ourselves to meditate?

Somehow, at the deepest level, you must make it your highest priority, third only to breathing and eating.

This is most important.

Nothing else will do.

It can enhance every aspect of life.

Have the discipline.

Allow yourself to be compelled.

Make those times inviolate.

Do it for yourself, your loved ones, the world.

Motivate yourself in whatever way you can.

It's the best habit you can have.

The second most important thing is to discard everything you think you know about how meditation is supposed to go.

Most people think they can't meditate. This is because they have ideas of what's supposed to happen—notably, "I'm supposed to quiet my mind."

This is hogwash.

Silence, or the 'no-thought' state, *can* occur during meditation from time to time. It can also occur at other times.

But the more we fight for it, the less it is likely to happen. It's not the goal of meditation, nor is it a skill we must cultivate. It's a lovely byproduct we can't directly control. It might arise but is not necessary.

One thing that always happens when anyone meditates, if they sit with their eyes closed and direct their attention inward, is just that. One's awareness is turned from the outer world of the senses towards the world of inner experience.

This might not always be pleasant, but if you just do it and be with what's within, it, alone, is healing.

In this meditation, we don't do much.

We set up the preconditions to bring about things our small will or self cannot.

We open the door for miracles that the surface levels of being cannot create.

We step aside and do the simplest thing we can to allow profound things to occur.

The less we go for any particular thing, the more potential there is for good.

Our job is to make it as easy as we can, to accept what is happening, to let go of effort and judgment and to relax and surrender.

It's in this simple state of accepting awareness, with the non-directed thought 'I love you and forgive you' coming in the easiest possible way, that allows for the higher knowing to take over and work its wonders.

It's not 'you' that's doing this. It's something much deeper than the mind, will or ego, something far more effective.

You're not using your mind to tell yourself, 'I love you and forgive you.' You're giving your mind something to do in repeating a string of words.

Think them lightly, as if they have no meaning. Don't grip them with your mind and beat yourself with them. And don't worry about always keeping them going.

When you remember, think them easily. Utilized in this way, they become like a submarine, carrying you, without your knowing, into the deeper reaches of your inner world where your higher power can deliver them to your deepest wounding.

Again, it's not you doing. It's the art of letting go while giving your mind the simplest thing to do with the most potential for healing.

It's opening the door to your inner wisdom, which cannot be forced, controlled or commanded. You are simply giving it the best scenario so it can bring about what you cannot.

If you find yourself struggling, the instruction is simple.

Stop struggling.

If you are, it's probably based on a misunderstanding. You are trying to quiet your mind or keep the mantra going or sit up straight. You're concerned about who's being forgiven. You're mad because you didn't do anything that needs forgiving. You have unmet expectations.

A friend of mine read the words of an Indian saint named Ramana Maharshi stating that he experienced God in every meditation.

Thereafter, my friend struggled with each different meditation he tried, including this one.

The point is our mind/ego/conditioning is endlessly clever at sabotaging us, coming up with excuses, 'ruining' our meditations, making us believe that we can't meditate in the first place.

It doesn't want us to heal.

It wants to maintain its grip.

It fears its death in our liberation.

But we can simply bypass it.

The irony is that when we do, when we use our will to get ourselves to meditate and accept each meditation as utterly perfect, then each one will move us closer to God, the basis of life, our own divine blueprint.

In this meditation, things are supposed to be exactly as they are. You're supposed to let your mind do whatever it needs to do. You're not supposed to continually try to keep the mantra going. You're supposed to sit comfortably and shift your position to be more comfortable. You can open your eyes from time to time and close them again if you're so moved.

Just don't get up and walk around or engage in other activity. The more the metabolism can settle down, the better. And it's best to let go of judging.

And when you remember, easily think 'I love you and forgive you.'

That's it.

Simplicity and power.

Relax. Take it easy. Be with what is. Even if you have innumerable mundane thoughts and only think the mantra a dozen times in a meditation, you've done it perfectly. Different experiences will occur over time.

One thing that can sometimes help is to shorten the mantra to 'love.'

If, when you begin, your mind is racing and you feel wired, think 'love' rapidly. After a few minutes, things will probably settle down. Then you can begin the longer mantra. From time to time, if needed, you could do this in the middle of the meditation, as well.

So let's say you're having a lot of thoughts and feeling restless. Take a deep breath and allow it. Even while the mind is having other thoughts, you can sometimes think 'I love you and forgive you' or start to think 'love' quickly, not as a bat to beat down whatever else the mind is doing, but as a simple practice that just might have some deeper value. And then just let go and stop trying to do anything for a while. Be aware of your inner experience. Then come back to 'I love you and forgive you.'

The little healings that happen in every meditation are imperceptible and accrue over time. Each session will have value. If we look for big things, we only frustrate ourselves. They, too, will come and not through our trying.

6. THE NITTY GRITTY

Memorize 'I love you and forgive you.'

Use it as it is.

If you're going to do this, do it as optimally as possible.

There are good reasons for the wording.

And the more of us doing this one, identical thing, the more we will influence the world for good.

Ultimately, there is only one I, the great I of I Am.

We are all parts of that.

So it's better not to repeat 'I' in the middle of the sentence.

This will help the small I step aside and the big I take over. Without trying, you become your higher power and start bestowing the healing energies of love and forgiveness where they are needed.

Likewise, there are two yous because there are innumerable ones that need healing, both within and without.

So sit comfortably with back support and your head free. Close your eyes and allow your awareness to be inward directed and, when you remember, easily think 'I love you and forgive you.'

If English is not your most natural language, translate the sentence into your own.

Utterly simple.

If you consciously try to bring anything else about you will just be getting in your own way.

The three times to meditate are shortly after awakening, before dinner and just before sleep.

This clears the night energies and sets up your day, clears the day energies and sets up your evening and clears the evening energies and sets up your night.

It also helps adjust and balance mood, physiology, hormones and metabolism.

I do thirty minutes in the morning, around twenty in the late afternoon and anywhere from a few minutes to fifteen or twenty sitting up in bed till I start to feel sleepy.

In the morning, I time myself with a clock. For the others, I don't.

Sometimes I go over. I rarely do less. This is the optimum.

But if you must, cut it down to as little as fifteen minutes in the morning and the afternoon. Any less won't do and twenty is far better than fifteen.

Every once in a while, do a longer meditation.

And occasional meditation retreats can work wonders.

If I awaken in the middle of the night and don't soon fall back to sleep, I sit up and meditate then as well. I have one pillow for sleeping and a firm one for leaning up against the wall.

Devote your full self to each meditation as much as possible, no matter what the experience may be.

Be gentle with yourself.

Accept what is.

If many of your meditations are a lot of mundane thoughts, so be it.

That's what your body/mind needs.

Over time you will begin to feel more of the qualities of the basis of life.

You are that.

It will begin to come forth.

Sometimes you might notice the mantra elongating, attenuating, getting softer and more abstract, the words becoming more wave-like, like marshmallows. This is an indication your awareness is sinking deeper. But don't look for this or try to make it happen. Just think the words easily as they come. Sometimes they may come faster, sometimes slower. It's all as perfect as it can be.

Sometimes difficult material might arise—fear, frustration, pain, terror, loneliness, grief, whatever.

This is simply old or fresh wounding needing to be released.

Whatever arises, no matter how difficult, allow it to fully be there and flow through you in whatever form it takes.

If it's crying, cry.

If it's terror or rage, feel it.

Perhaps in some life you were burned at the stake.

Perhaps as an infant you felt your life threatened.

That was then, this is now.

What was too difficult to fully face *can and must be faced now* if it spontaneously arises.

It's good that it's coming up.

Help it heal by fully meeting it.

Don't let the fear of fear, pain or death drive you away from it.

Turn towards it, fully embrace it, sit in the heart of it.

When we're in it, it feels like we have an infinite amount of pain.

We don't.

The more we let it arise and flow through us, the more is released.

This is the healing process.

Allow and be with whatever arises.

It will subside.

This goes for in meditation and out.

We don't need to go looking for it.

But if it comes, it's good.

It's natural to want to avoid it.

Do the opposite.

Be with it as long as it takes.

7. GOING WITHIN

We can improve our lives, our hearts and our habits.

When we do, we improve all that is.

We are here to learn and grow.

This is our deeper purpose.

The best way to progress on an even keel is to create a balance of inward and outward development.

In the East, the inner has been emphasized to the detriment of the outer.

Here in the West, it has been the opposite.

We are not used to going within.

We often don't appreciate that we can develop our inner world.

This notion is foreign to us.

But, ultimately, our soul is more important than our body or material circumstances.

Our growth, our evolution and the development of our awareness and being are what we carry forward.

We are built to go within.

Most people don't believe this, but it's true.

We already contain the natural tendency to dive deeply into our inner universe.

Meditating three times a day and doing what we do the rest of the time is the optimum balance of life and will lead to our optimum total development.

We can live love, freedom and wholeness.

Not because someone desirable might love us or we've just won the lottery but because love and gladness are pouring forth from the wellsprings of our being.

Not many of us live this.

We live something else.

Lack, resignation, defeat.

Anger, fear, greed.

Loss, sorrow, emptiness.

Whatever you may be living, you can come to live love.

And it's infinitely better than self-aggrandizement or self-abnegation.

We'll all have our ups and downs. We'll all have our difficult times.

But this is important.

At the core, at its most fundamental levels, life is love, simplicity and power; freedom, support and well being.

It's full, rich and vibrant.

These are its basic qualities.

Its nasty sides arise due to damage, distortion and pollution.

Trauma and assault turn wholeness into turmoil.

And there has been a great deal of this.

Untold horror, torture and devastation.

So we live pain, fear and dysfunction.

Somewhere within us we know we're not whole.

We're shattered and lost.

We have a hole in our being.

We've lost our divinity, our oneness with God.

For some of us this is more conscious than for others.

But most of us carry this deep within.

So logic demands that we have a reason.

We must have done something terribly wrong.

We must have sinned.

We carry the story of Adam and Eve.

Not that we ate an apple, but that we defied God and lost heaven.

This is a lie, but a lie we all carry.

We experience that we're not whole and free.

Therefore we must have done wrong.

It's true we're not living the grace that we can.

We live limitation and shadow.

Look around.

As a species, we're totally insane.

War is insane.

War is barbaric.

So we embrace perpetual war and destroy our food chain and habitat.

All because we live the unhealed state.

But our wounding isn't infinite.

It can be healed and released.

And as this occurs, life's true nature comes forth.

The love and simplicity.

The fullness and vibrancy.

Our own innate wisdom and wholeness.

Our divine blueprint.

And with this comes gratitude and fulfilling life.

—

Meditation can help.

Most meditations come from specific religions. This limits their use. And they don't utilize the deepest, most healing properties of love, forgiveness, simplicity and power. This limits their efficacy and can make them more difficult.

The Love and Forgiveness Meditation doesn't have these problems. It's new and secular, though love and forgiveness are at the heart of most religions. It's easy and accessible. And almost anyone can do it if they decide to and understand the foundations contained in this book.

It has the potential to heal.

Every time we do it, we benefit our world.

In imperceptible ways, it pours grace into everything.

We become the solution instead of the problem, an influence for good.

And if you already are a positive force in the world, it can help that flower even more.

We eat food three times a day.

Eat love and freedom three times a day.

It's more important than food, though we survive without it.

But at what cost?

Join us.

Try it for a year or the rest of your life.

It could open doors for miracles to occur.

It could help heal our world.

It could help save our lives.

It's what we can do.

8. DISCLAIMER

This is an alternative healing practice. I make no guarantees to anyone regarding results. I consider it the highest gift.

Belief is not required.

But still, an open heart and mind will yield the best results.

I welcome your input and feedback.

I invite you to experience for yourself.

ABOUT THE AUTHOR

After devoting a lifetime to healing and awakening himself and others utilizing therapy, many meditations, energy and bodywork, 12-step programs, Rebirthing, Shamanic Journey, Soul Retrieval, DNA Activation, Sacred Spirit Healing and esoteric Hindu, Vedic, Buddhist, Christian, Jewish, Hawaiian and Native-American practices, and, ultimately, pretty much giving up on attaining his goal for himself, Mark Landau was gifted with divine guidance to co-create the tool that healed what nothing else could. He has a Masters Degree in Linguistics and ordination as an Interfaith Minister and Spiritual Counselor and facilitates highest dimensional healing circles and individual sessions. He worked very closely with Maharishi Mahesh Yogi, founder of Transcendental Meditation, and studied and worked with four other teachers. By 2002, he had worked with thousands of people worldwide and had a growing following as a spiritual teacher. But his inner life didn't reflect this, so he stopped. On 4/29/12, he discovered the Love and Forgiveness Meditation. He lives in Santa Fe. For his other offerings, see www.mark-landau.com.

13890712R00027

Printed in Great Britain
by Amazon.co.uk, Ltd.,
Marston Gate.